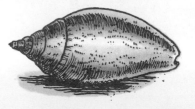

ACKNOWLEDGMENTS The editor and publisher have made every effort to trace the ownership of all copyrighted material and to secure permission from holders of such poems. In the event of any question arising as to the use of any material, the publisher and editor, while expressing regret for inadvertent error, will be pleased to make the necessary corrections in future printings. Thanks are due to the following authors, publishers, publications, and agents for permission to use the material indicated.

Appleton-Century-Crofts, Inc., for "The Elf and the Dormouse" by Oliver Herford, from *St. Nicholas Magazine,* 1901. Reprinted courtesy of Appleton-Century-Crofts, Inc.

Atheneum Publishers, Inc., for "Snowy Morning," copyright © 1969 by Lilian Moore from I THOUGHT I HEARD THE CITY; for "Wind Song," text copyright © 1967 by Lilian Moore from I FEEL THE SAME WAY. Both poems used by permission of Atheneum Publishers.

The Bodley Head Ltd., for "I Meant To Do My Work Today" from THE LONELY DANCER AND OTHER POEMS by Richard LeGallienne.

Jonathan Cape Ltd., for "Fog" from CHICAGO POEMS by Carl Sandburg. Reprinted by permission of Laurence Pollinger Limited.

Elizabeth Coatsworth for "The Country Cat."

Dodd, Mead & Company, Inc., for "I Meant To Do My Work Today" from THE LONELY DANCER AND OTHER POEMS by Richard LeGallienne, copyright 1913 by Dodd, Mead & Company; copyright renewed 1941 by Richard LeGallienne. Reprinted by permission of Dodd, Mead & Company, Inc.

Kenneth Durant for "Millions of Strawberries" by Genevieve Taggard, originally published in *The New Yorker.*

Grosset & Dunlap, Inc., for "Leave Me Alone," reprinted from AT THE TOP OF MY VOICE AND OTHER POEMS by Felice Holman. Copyright © 1970 by Felice Holman. A W. W. Norton Book published by Grosset & Dunlap, Inc.

Harcourt Brace Jovanovich, Inc., for "Listening" and "Trees" from THE LITTLE HILL by Harry Behn, copyright © 1949 by Harry Behn; for "Questions at Night" by Louis Untermeyer from RAINBOW IN THE SKY, edited by Louis Untermeyer, copyright © 1935 by Harcourt Brace Jovanovich, Inc.; renewed 1963 by Louis Untermeyer. All of these poems reprinted by permission of Harcourt Brace Jovanovich, Inc.

Harper & Row, Publishers, Inc., for "Rudolph Is Tired of the City" and "Keziah" from BRONZEVILLE BOYS AND GIRLS by Gwendolyn Brooks, copyright © 1956 by Gwendolyn Brooks Blakely. Reprinted by permission of Harper & Row, Publishers, Inc.

David Higham Associates, Ltd., for "Minnie" and "Griselda" from POEMS FOR CHILDREN by Eleanor Farjeon.

Holt, Rinehart and Winston, Inc., for "Fog" from CHICAGO POEMS by Carl Sandburg, copyright 1916 by Holt, Rinehart and Winston, Inc.; copyright © 1944 by Carl Sandburg. Reprinted by permission of Holt, Rinehart and Winston, Inc.

J. B. Lippincott Company, for "Is This Someone You Know?" and "Someone Slow" from YOU KNOW WHO by John Ciardi, copyright © 1964 by John Ciardi; for "Minnie" and "Griselda," copyright 1938 by Eleanor Farjeon. Renewal, ©, 1966 by Gervase Farjeon. From the book POEMS FOR CHILDREN by Eleanor Farjeon, copyright © 1951 by Eleanor Farjeon. All of these poems reprinted by permission of J. B. Lippincott Company.

Little, Brown and Company, for "The Tale of Custard the Dragon" from VERSES FROM 1929 ON by Ogden Nash, copyright © 1936 by Ogden Nash. Reprinted by permission of Little, Brown and Company.

The Macmillan Company, for "The Moon's the North Wind's Cooky" from COLLECTED POEMS by Vachel Lindsay, copyright 1914 by The Macmillan Company; renewed 1942 by Elizabeth C. Lindsay. Reprinted by permission of The Macmillan Company.

The New Yorker Magazine, Inc., for "Millions of Strawberries" by Genevieve Taggard, copyright © 1929, 1957 by The New Yorker Magazine, Inc. Reprinted by permission of The New Yorker Magazine, Inc., and Kenneth Durant.

Laurence Pollinger Limited, for "Fog" from CHICAGO POEMS by Carl Sandburg, published by Jonathan Cape Ltd. Reprinted by permission of Laurence Pollinger Limited.

Charles Scribner's Sons, for "The Fly-Away Horse" from POEMS OF CHILDHOOD by Eugene Field (Charles Scribner's Sons 1904). Reprinted courtesy of Charles Scribner's Sons.

The Society of Authors, for "Tartary" and "Silver" from COLLECTED POEMS by Walter de la Mare. Reprinted by permission of The Literary Trustees of Walter de la Mare, and The Society of Authors as their representatives.

The Viking Press, Inc., for "The Hens" from UNDER THE TREE by Elizabeth Madox Roberts, copyright 1922 by B. W. Huebsch, Inc.; renewed 1950 by Ivor S. Roberts. Reprinted by permission of The Viking Press, Inc.

THE GOLDEN BOOK OF POEMS

FOR THE VERY YOUNG

Selected by Louis Untermeyer | Pictures by Joan Walsh Anglund

GOLDEN PRESS • NEW YORK
WESTERN PUBLISHING COMPANY, INC.

CONTENTS

Library of Congress Catalog Card Number: 71-142154
Copyright © 1971, 1959 by Western Publishing Company, Inc.
Printed in the U.S.A. All rights reserved.
GOLDEN, A GOLDEN FAVORITE, and GOLDEN PRESS® are trademarks of
Western Publishing Company, Inc.

Spring

Sound the flute!
Now it's mute.
Birds delight
Day and Night;
Nightingale
In the dale,
Lark in Sky,
Merrily,
Merrily, merrily, to welcome in the Year.

Little Boy,
Full of joy;
Little Girl,
Sweet and small;
Cock does crow,
So do you;
Merry voice,
Infant noise,
Merrily, merrily, to welcome in the Year.

Little Lamb
Here I am;
Come and lick
My white neck;
Let me pull
Your soft Wool;
Let me kiss
Your soft face;
Merrily, merrily, we welcome in the Year.

William Blake

Millions of Strawberries

Marcia and I went over the curve,
Eating our way down
Jewels of strawberries we didn't deserve,
Eating our way down,
Till our hands were sticky, and our lips painted.
And over us the hot day fainted,
And we saw snakes,
And got scratched,
And a lust overcame us for the red unmatched
Small buds of berries,
Till we lay down—
Eating our way down—
And rolled in the berries like two little dogs,
Rolled
In the late gold.
And gnats hummed,
And it was cold,
And home we went, home without a berry,
Painted red and brown,
Eating our way down.

Genevieve Taggard

A Calendar

January brings the snow,
Makes our feet and fingers glow.

February brings the rain,
Thaws the frozen lake again.

March brings breezes, loud and shrill,
To stir the dancing daffodil.

April brings the primrose sweet,
Scatters daisies at our feet.

May brings flocks of pretty lambs
Skipping by their fleecy dams.

June brings tulips, lilies, roses,
Fills the children's hands with posies.

Hot July brings cooling showers,
Apricots, and gillyflowers.

August brings the sheaves of corn,
Then the harvest home is borne.

Warm September brings the fruit;
Sportsmen then begin to shoot.

Fresh October brings the pheasant;
Then to gather nuts is pleasant.

Dull November brings the blast;
Then the leaves are whirling fast.

Chill December brings the sleet,
Blazing fire, and Christmas treat.

Sara Coleridge

Pirate Story

Three of us afloat in the meadow by the swing,
    Three of us aboard in the basket on the lea.
Winds are in the air, they are blowing in the spring;
    And waves are on the meadow like the waves there are at sea.

Where shall we adventure, to-day that we're afloat,
    Wary of the weather and steering by a star?
Shall it be to Africa, a-steering of the boat,
    To Providence, or Babylon, or off to Malabar?

Hi! but here's a squadron a-rowing on the sea—
    Cattle on the meadow a-charging with a roar!
Quick, and we'll escape them, they're as mad as they can be,
    The wicket is the harbor and the garden is the shore.

Robert Louis Stevenson

Trees

Trees are the kindest things I know,
They do no harm, they simply grow

And spread a shade for sleepy cows,
And gather birds among their boughs.

They give us fruit in leaves above,
And wood to make our houses of,

And leaves to burn on Hallowe'en,
And in the Spring new buds of green.

They are the first when day's begun
To touch the beams of morning sun,

They are the last to hold the light
When evening changes into night,

And when a moon floats on the sky
They hum a drowsy lullaby

Of sleepy children long ago...
Trees are the kindest things I know.

Harry Behn

Snowy Morning

Wake
gently this morning
to a different day.
Listen.

There is no bray
of buses,
no brake growls,
no siren howls and
no horns
blow.
There is only
the silence
of a city
hushed
by snow.

Lilian Moore

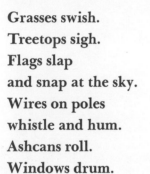

Wind Song

When the wind blows
The quiet things speak.
Some whisper, some clang,
Some creak.

Grasses swish.
Treetops sigh.
Flags slap
and snap at the sky.
Wires on poles
whistle and hum.
Ashcans roll.
Windows drum.

When the wind goes—
suddenly
then,
the quiet things
are quiet again.

Lilian Moore

11

The Moon's the North Wind's Cooky

The Moon's the North Wind's cooky.
He bites it, day by day,
Until there's but a rim of scraps
That crumble all away.

The South Wind is a baker.
He kneads clouds in his den,
And bakes a crisp new moon *that . . . greedy*
North . . . Wind . . . eats . . . again!

Vachel Lindsay

Silver

Slowly, silently, now the moon
Walks the night in her silver shoon;
This way, and that, she peers, and sees
Silver fruit upon silver trees;
One by one the casements catch
Her beams beneath the silvery thatch;
Couched in his kennel, like a log,
With paws of silver sleeps the dog;
From their shadowy cote the white breasts peep
Of doves in a silver-feathered sleep;
A harvest mouse goes scampering by,
With silver claws, and silver eye;
And moveless fish in the water gleam,
By silver reeds in a silver stream.

Walter de la Mare

Fog

The fog comes
on little cat feet.

It sits looking
over harbor and city
on silent haunches
and then moves on.

Carl Sandburg

The Little Elf

I met a little Elf-man, once,
  Down where the lilies blow.
I asked him why he was so small,
  And why he didn't grow.

He slightly frowned, and with his eye
  He looked me through and through.
"I'm quite as big for me," said he,
  "As you are big for you."

John Kendrick Bangs

The Elf and the Dormouse

Under a toadstool
Crept a wee elf
Out of the rain
To shelter himself.

Under the toadstool
Sound asleep
Sat a big dormouse
All in a heap.

Trembled the wee elf
Frightened, and yet
Fearing to fly away
Lest he got wet.

To the next shelter
Maybe a mile!
Sudden the wee elf
Smiled a wee smile,

Tugged till the toadstool
Toppled in two,
Holding it over him
Gaily he flew.

Soon he was safe home,
Dry as could be;
Soon woke the dormouse—
"Good gracious me!

"Where is my toadstool?"
Loud he lamented.

And that's how umbrellas
First were invented.

Oliver Herford

The City Mouse and the Garden Mouse

The city mouse lives in a house;
  The garden mouse lives in a bower,
He's friendly with the frogs and toads,
  And sees the pretty plants in flower.

The city mouse eats bread and cheese;
  The garden mouse eats what he can;
We will not grudge him seeds and stalks,
  Poor little, timid, furry man.

Christina Georgina Rossetti

The Hens

The night was coming very fast;
It reached the gate as I ran past.

The pigeons had gone to the tower of the church
And all the hens were on their perch,

Up in the barn, and I thought I heard
A piece of a little purring word.

I stopped inside, waiting and staying,
To try to hear what the hens were saying.

They were asking something, that was plain,
Asking it over and over again.

One of them moved and turned around,
Her feathers made a ruffled sound,

A ruffled sound, like a bushful of birds,
And she said her little asking words.

She pushed her head close into her wing,
But nothing answered anything.

Elizabeth Madox Roberts

Five Little Chickens

Said the first little chicken,
  With a queer little squirm,
"Oh, I wish I could find
  A fat little worm!"

Said the next little chicken,
  With an odd little shrug,
"Oh, I wish I could find
  A fat little bug!"

Said the third little chicken,
  With a sharp little squeal,
"Oh, I wish I could find
  Some nice yellow meal!"

Said the fourth little chicken,
  With a small sigh of grief,
"Oh, I wish I could find
  A green little leaf!"

Said the fifth little chicken,
  With a faint little moan,
"Oh, I wish I could find
  A wee gravel-stone!"

"Now, see here," said the mother,
  From the green garden-patch,
"If you want any breakfast,
  You must come and scratch."

The Swallow

Fly away, fly away, over the sea,
   Sun-loving swallow, for summer is done.
Come again, come again, come back to me,
   Bringing the summer and bringing the sun.

Christina Georgina Rossetti

The Caterpillar

Brown and furry
Caterpillar in a hurry;
Take your walk
To the shady leaf or stalk.

May no toad spy you,
May the little birds pass by you;
Spin and die,
To live again a butterfly.

Christina Georgina Rossetti

Lady-Bird

Lady-bird, lady-bird! fly away home!
   The field-mouse has gone to her nest,
The daisies have shut up their sleepy red eyes,
   And the bees and the birds are at rest.

   Lady-bird, lady-bird! fly away home!
      The glow-worm is lighting her lamp,
   The dew's falling fast, and your fine speckled wings
      Will flag with the close-clinging damp.

      Lady-bird, lady-bird! fly away home!
         The fairy bells tinkle afar!
      Make haste, or theyll catch you, and harness you fast
         With a cobweb, to Oberon's car.

Caroline Southey

16

The Owl

When cats run home and light is come,
    And dew is cold upon the ground,
And the far-off stream is dumb,
    And the whirring sail goes round,
    And the whirring sail goes round;
      Alone and warming his five wits,
    The white owl in the belfry sits.

When merry milkmaids click the latch,
    And rarely smells the new-mown hay,
And the cock hath sung beneath the thatch
    Twice or thrice his roundelay,
    Twice or thrice his roundelay;
      Alone and warming his five wits,
    The white owl in the belfry sits.

Alfred, Lord Tennyson

Happy Songs

Piping down the valleys wild,
    Piping songs of pleasant glee,
On a cloud I saw a child,
    And he, laughing, said to me,

"Pipe a song about a lamb,"
    So I piped with merry cheer;
"Piper, pipe that song again,"
    So I piped, he wept to hear.

"Drop thy pipe, thy happy pipe,
    Sing thy songs of happy cheer."
So I sang the same again,
    While he wept with joy to hear.

"Piper, sit thee down and write
    In a book that all may read."
So he vanish'd from my sight;
    And I pluck'd a hollow reed,

And I made a rural pen,
    And I stained the water clear,
And I wrote my happy songs
    Every child may joy to hear.

William Blake

The Snake

A narrow fellow in the grass
Occasionally rides;
You may have met him,—did you not,
His notice sudden is.

The grass divides as with a comb,
A spotted shaft is seen;
And then it closes at your feet
And opens further on.

He likes a boggy acre,
A floor too cool for corn.
Yet when a child, and barefoot,
I more than once, at morn,

Have passed, I thought, a whip-lash
Unbraiding in the sun,—
When, stooping to secure it,
It wrinkled, and was gone.

Several of nature's people
I know, and they know me;
I feel for them a transport
Of cordiality;

But never met this fellow,
Attended or alone,
Without a tighter breathing,
And zero at the bone.

Emily Dickinson

The Kitten Playing with the Falling Leaves

See the kitten on the wall
Sporting with the leaves that fall!
Withered leaves, one, two and three,
From the lofty elder-tree.
Through the calm and frosty air
Of this morning bright and fair
Eddying round and round they sink
Softly, slowly.—One might think,
From the motions that are made,
Every little leaf conveyed
Some small fairy, hither tending,
To this lower world descending.
—But the kitten how she starts!
Crouches, stretches, paws, and darts:
First at one, and then its fellow,
Just as light, and just as yellow:
There are many now—now one—
Now they stop and there are none.
What intentness of desire
In her up-turned eye of fire!
With a tiger-leap half way,
Now she meets the coming prey.
Lets it go at last, and then
Has it in her power again.

William Wordsworth

Country Cat

"Where are you going, Mrs. Cat,
　All by your lonesome lone?"
"Hunting a mouse, or maybe a rat
　Where the ditches are overgrown."

"But you're very far from your house and home,
　You've come a long, long way—"
"The further I wander, the longer I roam
　The more I find mice at play."

"But you're very near to the dark pinewood
　And foxes go hunting too."
"I know that a fox might find me good,
　But what is a cat to do?

"I have my kittens who must be fed,
　I *can't* have them skin and bone!"
And Mrs. Cat shook her brindled head
And went off by her lonesome lone.

Elizabeth Coatsworth

19

Rudolph Is Tired of the City

These buildings are too close to me.
I'd like to PUSH away.
I'd like to live in the country,
And spread my arms all day.

I'd like to spread my breath out, too—
As farmers' sons and daughters do.

I'd tend the cows and chickens.
I'd do the other chores.
Then, all the hours left I'd go
A-SPREADING out-of-doors.

Gwendolyn Brooks

Leave Me Alone

Loving care!
Too much to bear.
Leave me alone!

Don't brush my hair,
Don't pat my head,
Don't tuck me in
Tonight in bed,
Don't ask me if I want a sweet,
Don't fix my favorite things to eat,
Don't give me lots of good advice,
And most of all just don't be nice.

But when I've wallowed well in sorrow,
Be nice to me again tomorrow.

Felice Holman

Keziah

I have a secret place to go.
Not anyone may know.

And sometimes when the wind is rough
I cannot get there fast enough.

And sometimes when my mother
Is scolding my big brother,

My secret place, it seems to me,
Is quite the only place to be.

Gwendolyn Brooks

Someone Slow

I know someone who is so slow
It takes him all day and all night to go
From Sunday to Monday, and all week long
To get back to Sunday. He never goes wrong.
And he never stops. But oh, my dear,
From birthday to birthday it takes him all year!
And that's much too slow, as I know you know.
One day I tried to tell him so.
But all he would say was "tick" and "tock."

—Poor old slow GRANDFATHER CLOCK.

John Ciardi

21

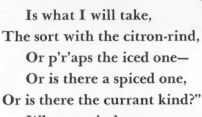

Minnie

Minnie can't make her mind up,
Minnie can't make up her mind!
   They ask her at tea,
    "Well, what shall it be?"
   And Minnie says, "Oh,
   Muffins, please! no,
   Sandwiches—yes,
   Please, egg-and-cress—
   I mean a jam one,
   Or is there a ham one,
Or is there another kind?
   Never mind!

   Cake
  Is what I will take,
The sort with the citron-rind,
   Or p'r'aps the iced one—
   Or is there a spiced one,
Or is there the currant kind?"
   When tea is done
   She hasn't begun,
She's always the one behind,
Because she can't make her mind up,
Minnie *can't* make up her mind!

Eleanor Farjeon

I Meant To Do My Work Today

I meant to do my work today—
But a brown bird sang in the apple tree,
And a butterfly flitted across the field,
And all the leaves were calling me.

And the wind went sighing over the land
Tossing the grasses to and fro,
And a rainbow held out its shining hand—
So what could I do but laugh and go?

Richard LeGallienne

Listening

I can hear kittens and cows and dogs
And cooing pigeons and grumpy frogs
And hundreds of pleasant far-off things
Like beetles snapping shut their wings
And chuffing trains and bells and walking
And people on the corner talking,

But when my mother calls to know
Why I'm so everlasting slow,
Or will I please stay off the lawn,
Or come and put my sweater on,
Then even when I'm very near
I honestly don't seem to hear.

Harry Behn

Griselda

Griselda is greedy, I'm sorry to say.
She isn't contented with four meals a day,
Like breakfast and dinner and supper and tea
(I've had to put tea after supper—you see
     Why, don't you?)
Griselda is greedy as greedy can be.

    She snoops about the larder
    For sundry small supplies,
    She breaks the little crusty bits
    Off rims of apple pies,
    She pokes the roast-potato-dish
    When Sunday dinner's done,
    And if there are two left in it
    Griselda snitches one;
    Cold chicken and cold cauliflower
    She pulls in little chunks—
And when Cook calls:
    "What *are* you doing there?"
    Griselda bunks.

Griselda is greedy. Well, that's how she feels,
She simply can't help eating in-between meals,
And always forgets what it's leading to, though
The Doctor has frequently told her: "You know
     Why, *don't* you?"
When the stomach-ache starts and Griselda says:
    "Oh!"

She slips down to the dining-room
When everyone's in bed,
For cheese-rind on the supper-tray,
And buttered crusts of bread,
A biscuit from the biscuit-box,
Lump sugar from the bowl,
A gherkin from the pickle-jar,
Are all Griselda's toll;
    She tastes the salted almonds,
    And she tries the candied fruits—
And when Dad shouts:
    "Who *is* it down below?"
    Griselda scoots.

Griselda is greedy. Her relatives scold,
And tell her how sorry she'll be when she's old,
She will lose her complexion, she's sure to grow fat,
She will spoil her inside—does she know what she's at?—
    (Why *do* they?)
Some people *are* greedy. Leave it at that.

Eleanor Farjeon

The Pobble Who Has No Toes

The Pobble who has no toes
    Had once as many as we;
When they said, "Some day you may lose them all;"
    He replied, "Fish fiddle de-dee!"
And his Aunt Jobiska made him drink
Lavender water tinged with pink;
For she said, "The World in general knows
There's nothing so good for a Pobble's toes!"

The Pobble who has no toes,
    Swam across the Bristol Channel;
But before he set out he wrapped his nose
    In a piece of scarlet flannel.
For his Aunt Jobiska said, "No harm
Can come to his toes if his nose is warm;
And it's perfectly known that a Pobble's toes
Are safe—provided he minds his nose."

The Pobble swam fast and well,
    And when boats or ships came near him,
He tinkledy-binkledy-winkled a bell
    So that all the world could hear him.
And all the Sailors and Admirals cried,
When they saw him nearing the further side,—
He has gone to fish, for his Aunt Jobiska's
Runcible Cat with crimson whiskers!"

But before he touched the shore,—
    The shore of the Bristol Channel,
A sea-green Porpoise carried away
    His wrapper of scarlet flannel.
And when he came to observe his feet,
Formerly garnished with toes so neat,
His face at once became forlorn
On perceiving that all his toes were gone!

And nobody ever knew,
    From that dark day to the present,
Whoso had taken the Pobble's toes,
    In a manner so far from pleasant.
Whether the shrimps or crawfish grey,
Or crafty Mermaids stole them away,
Nobody knew; and nobody knows
How the Pobble was robbed of his twice five toes!

The Pobble who has no toes
    Was placed in a friendly Bark,
And they rowed him back, and carried him up
    To his Aunt Jobiska's Park.
And she made him a feast, at his earnest wish,
Of eggs and buttercups fried with fish;
And she said, "It's a fact the whole world knows,
That Pobbles are happier without their toes."

Edward Lear

The Table and the Chair

Said the Table to the Chair,
"You can hardly be aware
How I suffer from the heat
And from chilblains on my feet.
If we took a little walk,
We might have a little talk;
Pray let us take the air,"
Said the Table to the Chair.

Said the Chair unto the Table,
"Now, you know we are not able:
How foolishly you talk,
When you know we cannot walk!"
Said the Table with a sigh,
"It can do no harm to try.
I've as many legs as you;
Why can't we walk on two?"

So they both went slowly down,
And walked about the town
With a cheerful bumpy sound
As they toddled round and round;

And everybody cried,
As they hastened to their side,
"See! the Table and the Chair
Have come out to take the air!"

But in going down an alley
To a castle in a valley,
They completely lost their way,
And wandered all the day;
Till, to see them safely back,
They paid a Ducky-quack,
And a Beetle, and a Mouse,
Who took them to their house.

Then they whispered to each other,
"O delightful little brother,
What a lovely walk we've taken!
Let us dine on beans and bacon."
So the Ducky and the leetle
Browny-Mousy *and* the Beetle
Dined and danced upon their heads
Till they toddled to their beds.

Edward Lear

Is This Someone You Know?

There was a boy who skinned his knees
Jumping over his father's trees.

He took a run and he took a jump,
And down he came with a skid and a bump.

The higher the trees the higher he jumped.
And when he came down the harder he bumped.

The harder he bumped the longer the skid.
But he jumped them all. He did, he did.

And every time he skinned his knees
He jumped again—as proud as you please.

Till he tried one day to jump over the sky.
But he

l
 a
  n
   d
    e
     d
      s
       o
hard it made him cry.

John Ciardi

The Tale of Custard the Dragon

Belinda lived in a little white house,
With a little black kitten and a little gray mouse,
And a little yellow dog and a little red wagon,
And a realio, trulio, little pet dragon.

Now the name of the little black kitten was Ink,
And the little gray mouse, she called her Blink,
And the little yellow dog was sharp as Mustard,
But the dragon was a coward, and she called him Custard.

Custard the dragon had big sharp teeth,
And spikes on top of him and scales underneath,
Mouth like a fireplace, chimney for a nose,
And realio, trulio daggers on his toes.

Belinda was as brave as a barrel-full of bears,
And Ink and Blink chased lions down the stairs,
Mustard was as brave as a tiger in a rage,
But Custard cried for a nice safe cage.

Belinda tickled him, she tickled him unmerciful,
Ink, Blink and Mustard, they rudely called him Percival,
They all sat laughing in the little red wagon
At the realio, trulio, cowardly dragon.

Belinda giggled till she shook the house,
And Blink said *Weeek!*, which is giggling for a mouse,
Ink and Mustard rudely asked his age,
When Custard cried for a nice safe cage.

Suddenly, suddenly they heard a nasty sound,
And Mustard growled, and they all looked around.
Meowch! cried Ink, and Ooh! cried Belinda,
For there was a pirate, climbing in the winda.

Pistol in his left hand, pistol in his right,
And he held in his teeth a cutlass bright;
His beard was black, one leg was wood.
It was clear that the pirate meant no good.

Belinda paled, and she cried Help! Help!
But Mustard fled with a terrified yelp,
Ink trickled down to the bottom of the household,
And little mouse Blink strategically mouseholed.

But up jumped Custard, snorting like an engine,
Clashed his tail like irons in a dungeon,
With a clatter and a clank and a jangling squirm
He went at the pirate like a robin at a worm.

The pirate gaped at Belinda's dragon,
And gulped some grog from his pocket flagon,
He fired two bullets, but they didn't hit,
And Custard gobbled him, every bit.

Belinda embraced him, Mustard licked him;
No one mourned for his pirate victim.
Ink and Blink in glee did gyrate
Around the dragon that ate the pyrate.

Belinda still lives in her little white house,
With her little black kitten and her little gray mouse,
And her little yellow dog and her little red wagon,
And her realio, trulio, little pet dragon.

Belinda is as brave as a barrel full of bears,
And Ink and Blink chase lions down the stairs,
Mustard is as brave as a tiger in a rage,
But Custard keeps crying for a nice safe cage.

Ogden Nash

27

The Owl and the Pussy-Cat

The Owl and the Pussy-Cat went to sea
   In a beautiful pea-green boat:
They took some honey, and plenty of money
   Wrapped up in a five-pound note.
The Owl looked up to the stars above,
   And sang to a small guitar,
"O lovely Pussy, O Pussy, my love,
   What a beautiful Pussy you are,
      You are,
      You are!
What a beautiful Pussy you are!"

Pussy said to the Owl, "You elegant fowl,
   How charmingly sweet you sing!
Oh! let us be married; too long we have tarried:
   But what shall we do for a ring?"
They sailed away, for a year and a day,
   To the land where the bong-tree grows;
And there in a wood a Piggy-wig stood,
   With a ring at the end of his nose,
      His nose,
      His nose,
With a ring at the end of his nose.

"Dear Pig, are you willing to sell for one shilling
   Your ring?" Said the Piggy, "I will."
So they took it away, and were married next day
   By the turkey who lives on the hill.
They dined on mince and slices of quince,
   Which they ate with a runcible spoon;
And hand in hand, on the edge of the sand,
   They danced by the light of the moon,
      The moon,
      The moon,
They danced by the light of the moon.

Edward Lear

Calico Pie

Calico Pie,
The little Birds fly
Down to the calico tree,
Their wings were blue,
And they sang "Tilly-loo!"
Till away they flew—
And they never came back to me!
They never came back!
They never came back!
They never came back to me!

Calico Jam,
The little Fish swam
Over the syllabub sea,
He took off his hat,
To the Sole and the Sprat,
And the Willeby-wat—
But he never came back to me!
He never came back!
He never came back!
He never came back to me!

Calico Ban,
The little Mice ran,
To be ready in time for tea,
Flippity flup,
They drank it all up,
And danced in the cup—
But they never came back to me!
They never came back!
They never came back!
They never came back to me!

Calico Drum,
The Grasshoppers come,
The Butterfly, Beetle, and Bee,
Over the ground,
Around and round,
With a hop and a bound—
But they never came back!
They never came back!
They never came back!
They never came back to me!

Edward Lear

The Land of Story-Books

At evening when the lamp is lit,
Around the fire my parents sit;
They sit at home and talk and sing,
And do not play at anything.

Now, with my little gun I crawl
All in the dark along the wall,
And follow round the forest track
Away behind the sofa back.

There, in the night, where none can spy,
All in my hunter's camp I lie,
And play at books that I have read
Till it is time to go to bed.

These are the hills, these are the woods,
These are my starry solitudes;
And there the river by whose brink
The roaring lions come to drink.

I see the others far away.
As if in firelit camp they lay,
And I, like to an Indian scout,
Around their party prowled about.

So, when my nurse comes in for me,
Home I return across the sea,
And go to bed with backward looks
At my dear land of Story-Books.

Robert Louis Stevenson

Questions at Night

Why
Is the sky?

What starts the thunder overhead?
Who makes the crashing noise?
Are the angels falling out of bed?
Are they breaking all their toys?

Why does the sun go down so soon?
Why do the night-clouds crawl
Hungrily up to the new-laid moon
And swallow it, shell and all?

If there's a Bear among the stars,
As all the people say,
Won't he jump over those pasture-bars
And drink up the Milky Way?

Does every star that happens to fall
Turn into a firefly?
Can't it ever get back to Heaven at all?
And why
Is the sky?

Louis Untermeyer

The Fly-Away Horse

Oh, a wonderful horse is the Fly-Away Horse—
    Perhaps you have seen him before;
Perhaps, while you slept, his shadow has swept
    Through the moonlight that floats on the floor.
For it's only at night, when the stars twinkle bright,
    That the Fly-Away Horse, with a neigh
And a pull at his rein and a toss of his mane,
    Is up on his heels and away!
        The Moon in the sky,
        As he gallopeth by,
Cries: "Oh! what a marvelous sight!"
        And the Stars in dismay
        Hide their faces away
In the lap of old Grandmother Night.

It is yonder, out yonder, the Fly-Away Horse
    Speedeth ever and ever away—
Over meadows and lanes, over mountains and plains,
    Over streamlets that sing at their play;
And over the sea like a ghost sweepeth he,
    While the ships they go sailing below,
And he speedeth so fast that the men at the mast
    Adjudge him some portent of woe.
        "What ho, there!" they cry,
        As he flourishes by
With a whisk of his beautiful tail;
        And the fish in the sea
        Are as scared as can be,
From the nautilus up to the whale!

And the Fly-Away Horse seeks those far-away lands
    You little folk dream of at night—
Where candy-trees grow, and honey-brooks flow,
    And corn-fields with popcorn are white;
And the beasts in the wood are ever so good
    To children who visit them there—
What glory astride of a lion to ride,
    Or to wrestle around with a bear!
      The monkeys, they say:
      "Come on, let us play,"
And they frisk in the coconut-trees:
      While the parrots, that cling
      To the peanut-vines, sing
Or converse with comparative ease!

Off! scamper to bed—you shall ride him to-night!
    For, as soon as you've fallen asleep,
With a jubilant neigh he shall bear you away
    Over forest and hillside and deep!
But tell us, my dear, all you see and you hear
    In those beautiful lands over there,
Where the Fly-Away Horse wings his far-away course
    With the wee one consigned to his care.
      Then grandma will cry
      In amazement: "Oh, my!"
And she'll think it could never be so.
      And only we two
      Shall know it is true—
You and I, little precious! shall know!

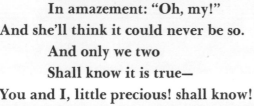

Eugene Field

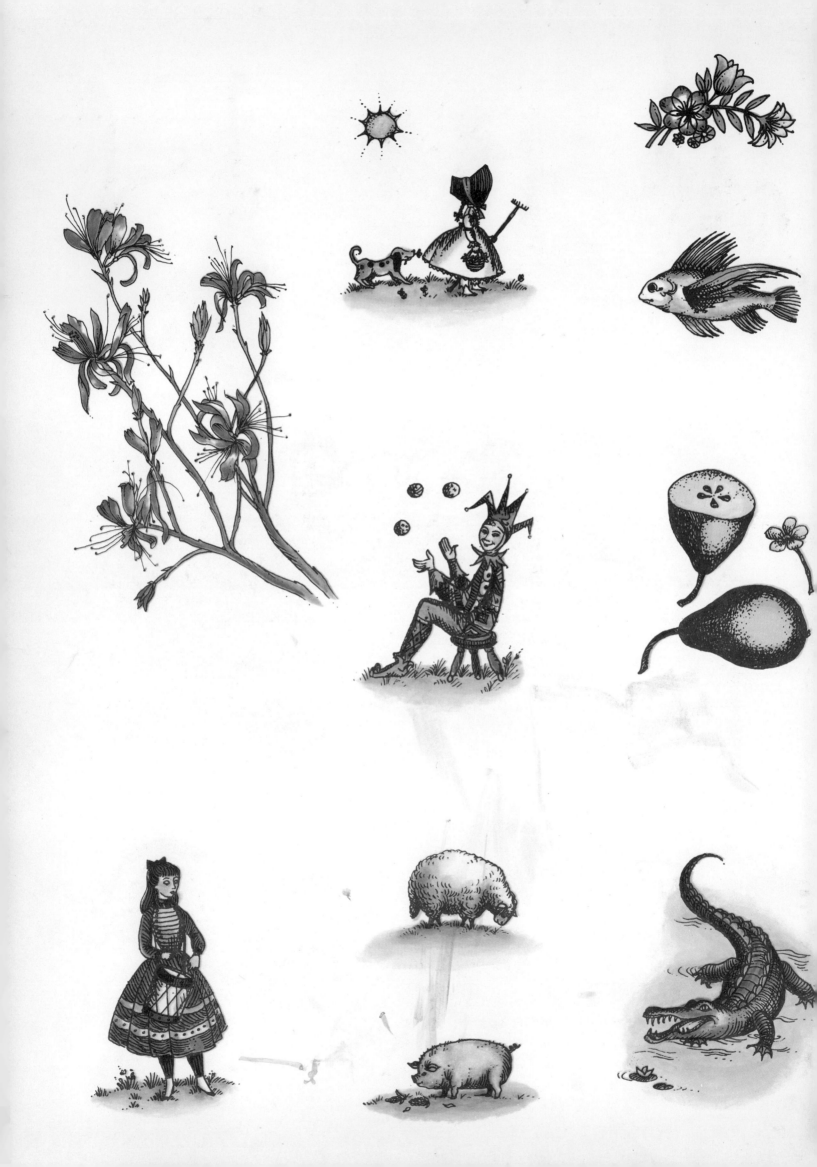